PLANTS BEGIN TO GROW ON LAND
470 MILLION YEARS AGO

THE FIRST REPTILES EVOLVE
312 MILLION YEARS AGO

FISH CRAWL ON TO
LAND 380 MILLION
YEARS AGO

THE FIRST FISH EVOLVE
525 MILLION YEARS AGO

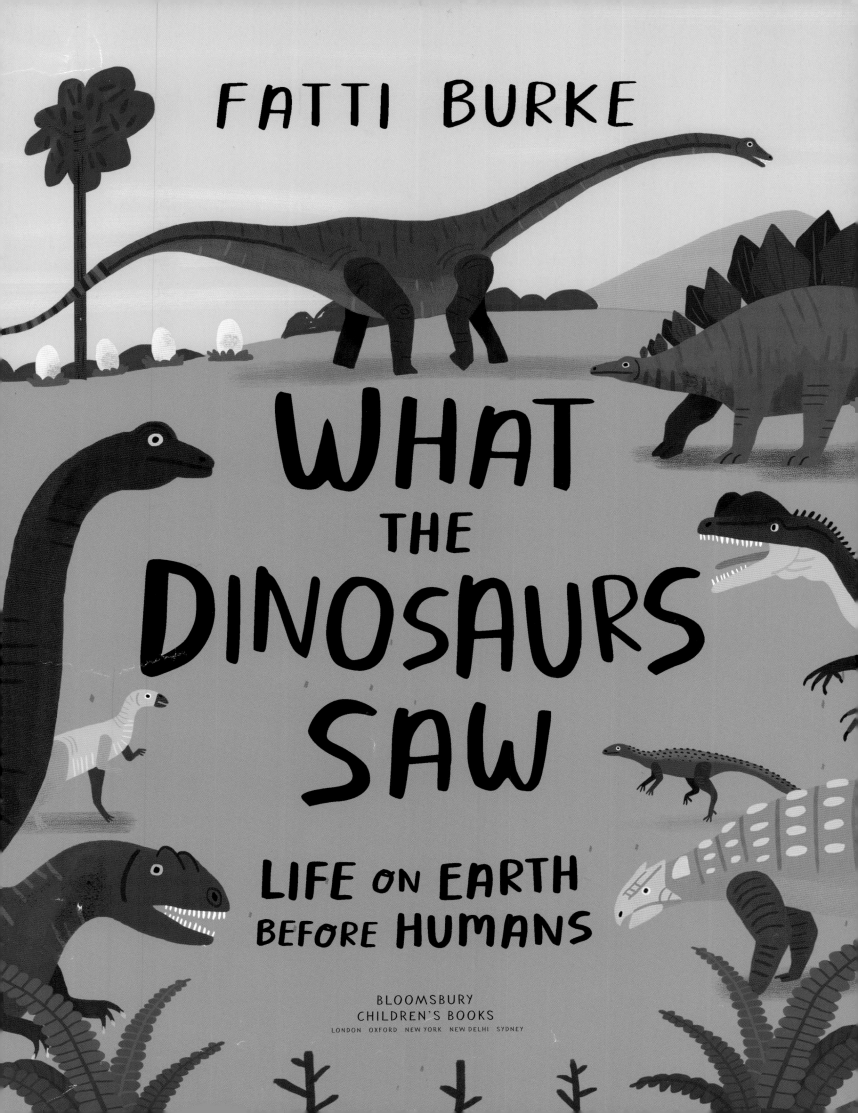

FATTI BURKE

WHAT THE DINOSAURS SAW

LIFE ON EARTH BEFORE HUMANS

BLOOMSBURY
CHILDREN'S BOOKS
LONDON OXFORD NEW YORK NEW DELHI SYDNEY

To my nephews, Sean and Finley. Of all the humans that have ever lived on our world, I think you guys are my favourite ones. I can't wait to watch how you change it for the better.

INTRODUCTION

Human beings like you and me have existed on Earth for around 200,000 years, and human-like ancestors were around for over two million years before that. This sounds like an unimaginable amount of time but there was a lot happening on planet Earth for over *four billion* years before we ever showed up!

There were huge volcanic eruptions and toxic smog filled the air. Deadly dinosaurs roamed the Earth, and all of the continents were joined together into one big piece. There were Ice Ages and meteors, underwater monsters and flying lizards.

The Earth certainly was a very different place back then. So, what exactly happened during all those years?

Let's find out!

It's hard to believe, but there was once a time
when everything was nothing. There was no
universe, no space – and even no time.

NOTHING.

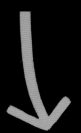

BIG BANG 13.6 BILLION YEARS AGO

THE BIG BANG

Our whole universe began as a tiny dot, smaller than this full stop. Smaller than anything you've ever seen in your life. This dot was filled with so much hot, dense energy that it burst and created the biggest event of all time – THE BIG BANG!

In a fraction of a millisecond, matter was created. Where once there was nothing, our universe had formed.

TODAY

THE UNIVERSE

Electrons, neutrons and protons all stuck together to form the building blocks of our universe – atoms. The simplest atom was hydrogen with just one proton and one electron.

NEUTRON

PROTON

ATOM

ELECTRON

Atoms combined and grew, releasing light and heat. Some of these atoms became stars, which became galaxies. Galaxies are collections of billions of stars. It took millions of years for all of these stars to form.

SUN

NEPTUNE

Our Sun and the planets that orbit it were created at roughly the same time, formed from atoms left over from other burned-out stars.

SATURN

MARS

VENUS

JUPITER

URANUS

EARTH

MERCURY

TIMELINE

STARS AND GALAXIES BEGIN
TO FORM 200 MILLION YEARS
AFTER THE BIG BANG

OUR SUN FORMS 4.6 BILLION
YEARS AGO

EARTH FORMS
4.5 BILLION YEARS AGO

PLANET EARTH

When Earth was first formed about 4.5 billion years ago, it was unrecognisable to the planet we live on today. Instead of land and water, the surface was covered in molten hot volcanic lava. Ouch! And instead of our long twenty-four-hour days, the Earth rotated so quickly that each day was only four hours long.

THEIA

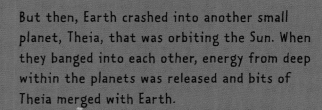

PROTO-EARTH

MILKY WAY

Our galaxy, the **MILKY WAY**, was formed around **200 MILLION YEARS** after the Big Bang.

But then, Earth crashed into another small planet, Theia, that was orbiting the Sun. When they banged into each other, energy from deep within the planets was released and bits of Theia merged with Earth.

EARTH

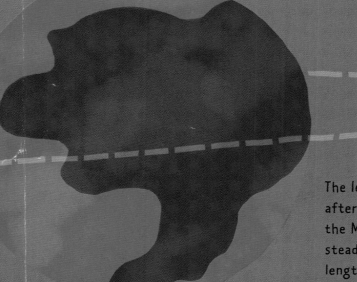

MOON

The leftover rubble floating around Earth after the collision stuck together to form the Moon. The gravitational pull of the Moon steadied Earth as it orbited the Sun and this lengthened the days, eventually becoming a lovely twenty-four hours.

GRAVITY is the force that pulls two objects together. The Sun's gravity makes the Earth revolve around it, and the Earth's gravity keeps the Moon in orbit and stops people from floating away.

TODAY

WATER AND AIR

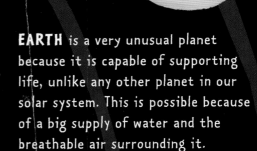

Half a billion years after forming, Earth's surface cooled down and hardened enough for liquids to settle on it. Water collected to create deep lakes, flowing rivers and vast oceans.

EARTH is a very unusual planet because it is capable of supporting life, unlike any other planet in our solar system. This is possible because of a big supply of water and the breathable air surrounding it.

WATER

ATMOSPHERE

VENUS would be a terrible planet for supporting life. Its surface is covered in volcanoes, the atmosphere is hot enough to melt lead and contains clouds of sulphuric acid.

MARS is the next best thing we have to Earth. It isn't too hot or too cold and its soil contains some water in the form of ice.

POISONOUS GASES

An atmosphere formed around Earth made from the gases spewed from volcanoes on its surface. These gases included methane, carbon dioxide and hydrogen sulphide. Poison to you and me.

TIMELINE

EARTH'S SURFACE BEGINS TO HARDEN AND OCEANS ARE FORMED 4 BILLION YEARS AGO

FRESH AIR

But how did these poisonous gases turn into the lovely clean air that makes Earth's atmosphere breathable? Well, tiny organisms called CYANOBACTERIA started growing in Earth's new oceans. These clever little blobs used the carbon dioxide in the water and turned it into oxygen – just like plants do – in a process called photosynthesis.

CYANOBACTERIA

SUN

WATER

OXYGEN

BLUE SKIES

Over time, the amount of oxygen in the atmosphere began to grow and grow, and about two billion years ago, the poisonous gases in Earth's atmosphere cleared up and the sky turned clear and blue.

In the stratosphere, oxygen atoms combined to create a new type of gas called ozone. A thin layer of ozone surrounds Earth and acts as an essential shield, protecting the planet and its inhabitants from the Sun's extremely dangerous Ultraviolet rays, which can cause damage to our skin and DNA.

EXOSPHERE

THERMOSPHERE

MESOSPHERE

STRATOSPHERE

TROPOSPHERE

OZONE

BACTERIA BEGIN TO PRODUCE
OXYGEN 2.4 BILLION YEARS AGO

EARLY SIGNS OF LIFE

Now that Earth had oxygen and plenty of water, it was ready for life. And just as the universe started off as a tiny dot, the first life on Earth came from very humble beginnings.

Earth was quite a violent place when life first began. Electrical storms filled the skies and volcanoes were erupting on the land.

Life may have begun in shallow puddles of water called **TIDAL POOLS,** which were full of something called primordial soup. Not as delicious as it sounds, primordial soup is the name given to the mixture of chemicals needed to create life.

TIDAL POOLS

Over many millions of years, as the ingredients of life splashed around together in the tidal pools, they formed the first single-cell organisms (like bacteria) about 3.5 billion years ago.

CHARNIA

More complicated forms of life took much longer to **EVOLVE,** with the first animals appearing another three billion years later! **CHARNIA** were early animals who lived on the ocean floor about 570 million years ago. Their bodies were shaped like quilted leaves, and they filtered their food from the water.

EVOLUTION is a theory used by scientists. It explains how living things change over a very long time, and how they have come to be the way they are.

TIMELINE

THE FIRST SINGLE-CELL ORGANISMS EVOLVE 3.5 BILLION YEARS AGO

THE FIRST ANIMALS

As the atmosphere became richer in oxygen, Earth became home to a diverse assortment of life forms that kept changing and adapting to their surroundings. This period is known as the CAMBRIAN EXPLOSION. It was the time when most types of animals appeared on Earth. Some of these types of animals were CHORDATES, BRACHIOPODS and ARTHROPODS.

CHORDATES have a nerve cord running down the length of their bodies, and often have a tail for at least some of their life cycle. An early chordate was the PIKAIA GRACILENS, a worm-like creature that lived in the sea.

PIKAIA GRACILENS

LINGULA

BRACHIOPODS live in shells and look a lot like clams or cockles. Some of the earliest brachiopods still exist today, like the LINGULA.

ARTHROPODS are creatures with hard skeletons on the outside of their bodies which provide support and also protect them from predators. Arthropods, like the TRILOBITE, are the ancestors of spiders, insects and crustaceans, like crabs and shrimp.

TRILOBITE

VERTEBRATES

After the Cambrian Explosion, the Earth's creatures continued to develop and change. About ten million years afterwards, a new type of animal started to appear. Vertebrates are descended from chordates and, today, include any animal that has a backbone, all mammals, birds, reptiles, amphibians and fish.

The first vertebrates, from the **MYLLOKUNMINGIA** and **HAIKOUICHTHYS** families, appeared around 525 million years ago. Like all forms of early life, they lived in the sea.

MYLLOKUNMINGIA FENGJIAOA looked a lot like a slug, and was about the size of a paperclip – less than three centimetres long. Unlike a slug (or a paperclip) it had a skull and a skeleton made of **CARTILAGE.**

Cartilage is a rubbery tissue that is softer than bone. Humans have it in their ears and noses, as well as in other parts of the body.

MYLLOKUNMINGIA

HAIKOUICHTHYS

HAIKOUICHTHYS ERCAICUNENSIS was a little bit smaller and narrower than Myllokunmingia. It had a tail that was distinctly separate from its body, and at least six gills on its head.

TIMELINE

THE FIRST FISH

Early fish didn't have jaws to eat with, so they stayed close to the seabed and used their gills to breathe and to suck up food. These jawless fish are called AGNATHA, and two types of these fish still exist today: LAMPREYS and HAGFISH.

LAMPREY

HAGFISH

LAMPREYS live deep down in the salty oceans or freshwaters of Europe, and HAGFISH can be found on the seabed across the world's oceans. All living and most extinct Agnatha do not have stomachs.

The scary-looking lamprey has a toothy, sucking mouth. Some lampreys bore into the flesh of other fish to suck their blood! Lazy lampreys also attach themselves to larger animals to get a free ride.

HAGFISH are sometimes called slime eels, because they produce a milky, sticky slime to defend themselves from being eaten. The first hagfish had basic vertebrae made from cartilage but they have evolved over time to not have any at all. This makes them the only known living animals that have a skull but no vertebrae.

FIRST VERTEBRATES APPEAR
525 MILLION YEARS AGO

TODAY

ARMOURED FISH

The problem with early jawless fish, like hagfish and lampreys, is that the soft cartilage in their bodies didn't fossilise well enough for scientists to study. This means that the oldest known fossilised fish skeletons belonged to a different sort of ancient jawless fish: Ostracoderms. The Ostracoderms existed alongside lamprey and hagfish, between 430 and 350 million years ago.

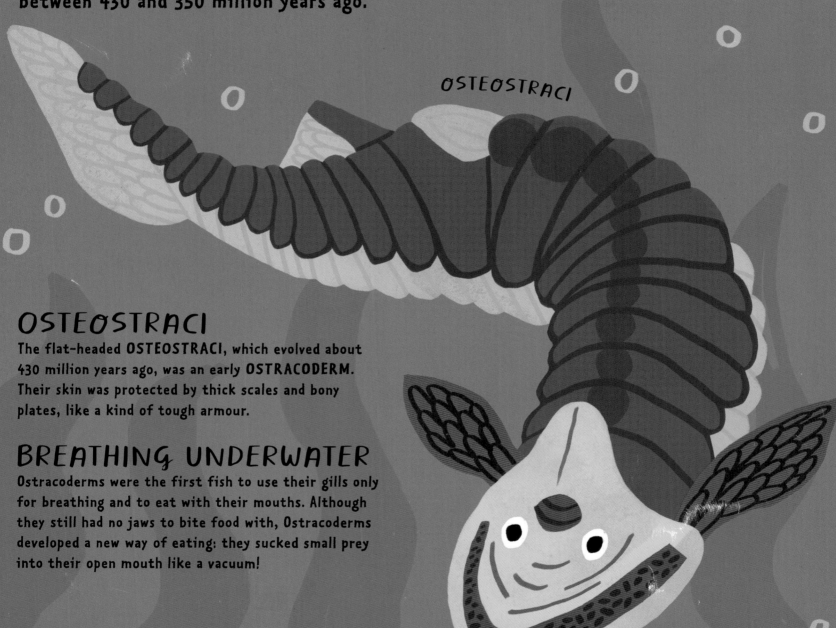

OSTEOSTRACI

OSTEOSTRACI

The flat-headed OSTEOSTRACI, which evolved about 430 million years ago, was an early OSTRACODERM. Their skin was protected by thick scales and bony plates, like a kind of tough armour.

BREATHING UNDERWATER

Ostracoderms were the first fish to use their gills only for breathing and to eat with their mouths. Although they still had no jaws to bite food with, Ostracoderms developed a new way of eating: they sucked small prey into their open mouth like a vacuum!

TIMELINE

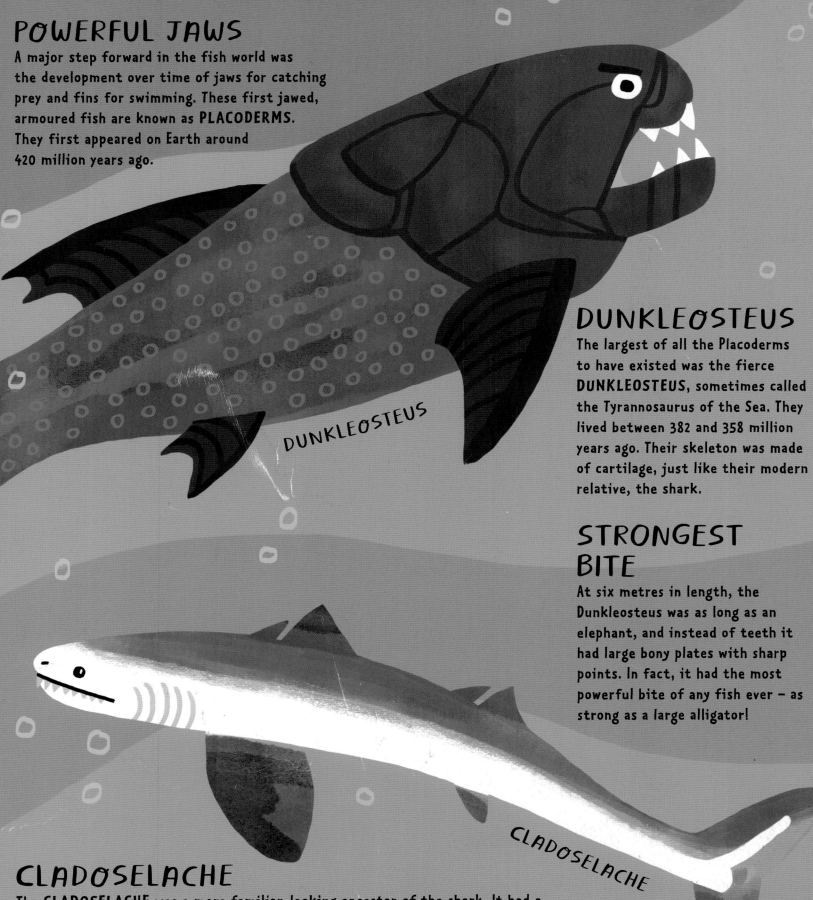

POWERFUL JAWS

A major step forward in the fish world was the development over time of jaws for catching prey and fins for swimming. These first jawed, armoured fish are known as PLACODERMS. They first appeared on Earth around 420 million years ago.

DUNKLEOSTEUS

DUNKLEOSTEUS

The largest of all the Placoderms to have existed was the fierce DUNKLEOSTEUS, sometimes called the Tyrannosaurus of the Sea. They lived between 382 and 358 million years ago. Their skeleton was made of cartilage, just like their modern relative, the shark.

STRONGEST BITE

At six metres in length, the Dunkleosteus was as long as an elephant, and instead of teeth it had large bony plates with sharp points. In fact, it had the most powerful bite of any fish ever – as strong as a large alligator!

CLADOSELACHE

CLADOSELACHE

The CLADOSELACHE was a more familiar-looking ancestor of the shark. It had a streamlined body, a rounded snout and no scales at all. Its teeth had lots of smooth ridges, making them perfect for biting and grasping but not for chewing. Therefore, they probably grabbed their prey by the tail and swallowed them whole – gulp!

TODAY

JAWED FISH EXISTED
420 MILLION YEARS AGO

INVERTEBRATES

As vertebrates were advancing 430 million years ago, so were the invertebrates. Invertebrates are animals *without* any backbone or skeleton. Instead, some have a strong outer shell to protect their soft bodies. Early invertebrates are ancestors of all the insects, molluscs, worms, jellyfish and crustaceans that make up 97% of animals on Earth today!

PTERYGOTUS was a sea scorpion that was bigger than a fully-grown human! Its sharp fangs looked like a lobster's claws, and it had strong paddles to help it swim in the sea and rivers.

PTERYGOTUS

TRILOBITES were related to woodlice and crabs. Their bodies were made up of lots of different segments, which allowed them to curl up for safety. There have been over 17,000 different types of trilobites, some as small as fleas and some as big as a dog!

STARFISH are invertebrates that date back 450 million years. They live in the sea and have five arms that grow out of a central disc where their organs are. These arms come in very handy. They can shed them as a form of defence, and can even regrow them!

TRILOBITE

TIMELINE

THE FIRST PLANTS

The first plants on Earth were types of algae (and later, moss) that grew in water. Then, around 470 million years ago, mosses and other plants began to grow on land.

MOSS

ALGAE

COOKSONIA

COOKSONIA were some of the first plants to grow on land. They were very small, just a couple of centimetres high, and had no leaves or flowers.

SPORES

TODAY

PLANTS GROW ON LAND 470 MILLION YEARS AGO

TETRAPODS AND AMPHIBIANS

Between about 380 and 340 million years ago, as the world continued to evolve, some fish crawled on to land for the first time in search of food or new pools of water. Have you ever seen a goldfish out of its bowl? Not the most graceful mover!

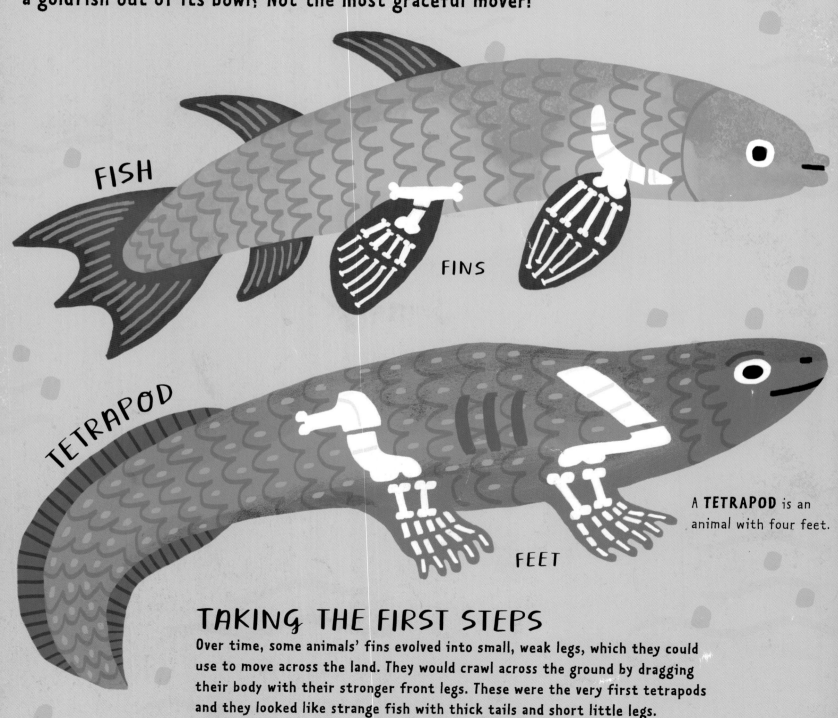

FISH

FINS

TETRAPOD

FEET

A **TETRAPOD** is an animal with four feet.

TAKING THE FIRST STEPS

Over time, some animals' fins evolved into small, weak legs, which they could use to move across the land. They would crawl across the ground by dragging their body with their stronger front legs. These were the very first tetrapods and they looked like strange fish with thick tails and short little legs.

TIKTAALIK

A **TIKTAALIK** is one of the creatures that shows this transition from swimming towards walking. It looked like a mix between a fish and a frog.

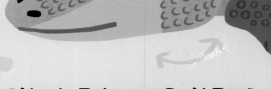

TIKTAALIK

SHAKE YOUR HEAD

Tiktaaliks developed little shoulders, arms and wrists, and their heads could turn from side to side (meaning that it most likely had the world's first neck!). The oldest Tiktaalik fossil is 375 million years old.

An **AMPHIBIAN** is a vertebrate that is born with gills for breathing underwater but develops lungs for breathing on land as an adult.

ICHTHYOSTEGA

ICHTHYOSTEGA

A later type of tetrapod that crawled its way from water to land was the **ICHTHYOSTEGA**. Although it had the long tail and gills of a fish, it also had lungs, and its skull and limbs looked more like a salamander's.

LAYING EGGS

Early amphibians would almost always have to return to the water to lay their eggs but were able to spend a lot more of their time on land because of their newly developed lungs.

EGGS

TODAY

AMPHIBIANS CRAWL ON TO LAND
380 MILLION YEARS AGO

REPTILES

For a long time, amphibians ruled the land, but there was one thing holding them back – they had to live near water to lay their eggs. In dry climates and inland, being able to survive on dry land would be a great advantage. And so, over 310 million years ago, some amphibians began to evolve into reptiles!

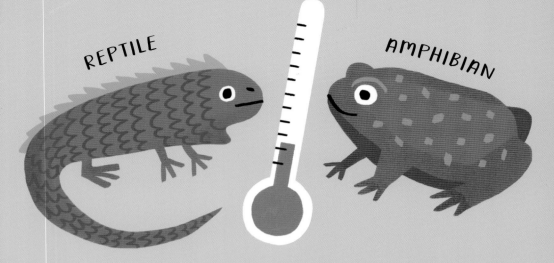

REPTILE

AMPHIBIAN

So, what's the difference between a reptile and an amphibian? Well, they're both **COLD-BLOODED**, which means that they don't generate heat inside their body. They need heat sources, like the Sun, to keep themselves warm.

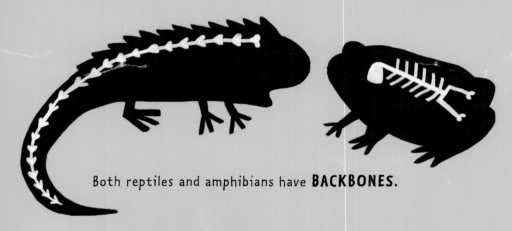

Both reptiles and amphibians have **BACKBONES**.

Reptiles lay **EGGS** with shells on land as opposed to amphibians, who lay shell-less eggs in water, like frogspawn.

SHELLED EGG

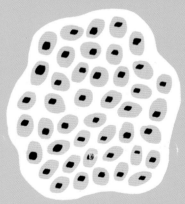

SHELL-LESS EGGS

Amphibians can **BREATHE** through their skin underwater. Most reptiles only breathe air through their lungs, and their thick, waterproof skin helps them store water inside their bodies to prevent them from drying out.

TIMELINE

18

EARLY REPTILES

Anapsids were reptiles with skulls that had no holes around the temple area.

HYLONOMUS

HYLONOMUS was an anapsid which lived about 312 million years ago. It is known as the first reptile ever to exist. At only 20 centimetres long, this tiny lizard-like creature had its pick of the insects and millipedes that lived on land.

ARAEOSCELIS

ARAEOSCELIS was a diapsid that lived 280 million years ago. At 60 centimetres long, this small reptile looked a lot like the little lizards that we see in pet shops and zoos today.

LATER REPTILES

Diapsids are reptiles that developed two skull holes behind each eye. These reptiles evolved to be dinosaurs, crocodiles, snakes, lizards, turtles and birds!

MAMMAL ANCESTORS

Synapsids evolved from early reptiles and are animals with one hole behind each eye socket in their skull. Early synapsids are the ancestors of all of today's mammals!

The Dimetrodon's sail was an extension of its spine and it may have helped it to attract a mate or acted as a solar panel which heated up its body early in the morning.

One of the most successful synapsids was the **DIMETRODON**, who lived from around 295 to 270 million years ago. It was a three-metre long giant lizard-like beast with a long, heavy tail and an impressive 'sail' on its back.

DIMETRODON

TODAY

SOME AMPHIBIANS EVOLVE INTO REPTILES 312 MILLION YEARS AGO

PANGAEA

If you look at a map of Earth today, you might notice that its seven continents (Africa, Antarctica, Asia, Europe, Oceania, North America and South America) look kind of like jigsaw pieces that could easily slot into each other.

ASIA

EUROPE

PANGAEA

NORTH AMERICA

CENTRAL AMERICA

SOUTH AMERICA

AFRICA

ASIA

OCEANIA

PANTHALASSA

ANTARCTICA

From about 300 to 180 million years ago, the seven continents on Earth were squished together as part of one supercontinent called **PANGAEA,** and the rest of the planet was one big ocean called **PANTHALASSA.**

Over time, this supercontinent broke apart, and the pieces of land slowly drifted away from one another. In fact, they're still drifting apart, so the way the Earth looks today is not how it will look forever.

TIMELINE

THE EARTH'S LAYERS

Earth is made up of three layers: the CORE, the MANTLE and the CRUST. The CORE is at the very centre and is about the same temperature as the surface of the Sun. The MANTLE is about 2,900 kilometres thick and separates the core from the crust. The CRUST sits on the mantle and is only between 8 to 32 kilometres thick. It is divided up into sections called PLATES.

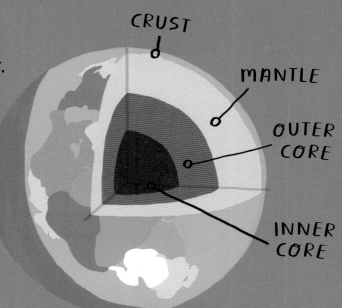

CRUST
MANTLE
OUTER CORE
INNER CORE

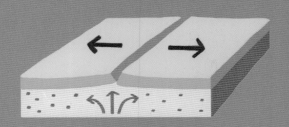

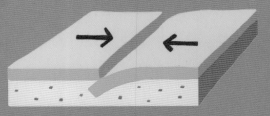

HOW DO THE CONTINENTS MOVE?

The Earth's super-hot core heats up the mantle from below, turning the rock into a lava-like liquid. This rises to the surface but can't get past the hard layer of crust. The plates of the crust, which sit on the mantle, float around on top and that's how the continents drift away from each other. This process happens very slowly though, with the plates only moving two centimetres every year. So, it took MILLIONS of years for Pangaea to break apart into the seven separate continents.

Where plates move apart and collide, natural disasters like earthquakes, volcanic eruptions and tsunamis can happen.

FREEZING

Pangaea would have been a tough place to live. The south of the continent was cold and dry, and some of it was frozen under ice caps.

SIZZLING

The northern and central parts were extremely hot and could be either very dry or completely flooded depending on the seasons.

DANGER!

As Earth's land masses were moving, they hit and scraped off one another, sometimes causing violent volcanic eruptions!

TODAY

EARTH HAD ONE SUPERCONTINENT BETWEEN 300–180 MILLION YEARS AGO

THE GREAT DYING

Try to imagine almost every species on Earth today becoming extinct. That is exactly what happened 252 million years ago in a terrible disaster known as the Great Dying.

EXTINCTION

Although nobody is certain what caused the Great Dying, it was probably brought on by the combination of dangerous chemicals in the atmosphere being spewed from Pangaea's erupting volcanos, the release of toxic gases from the sea floors, the low oxygen levels in the air and very hot, dry weather.

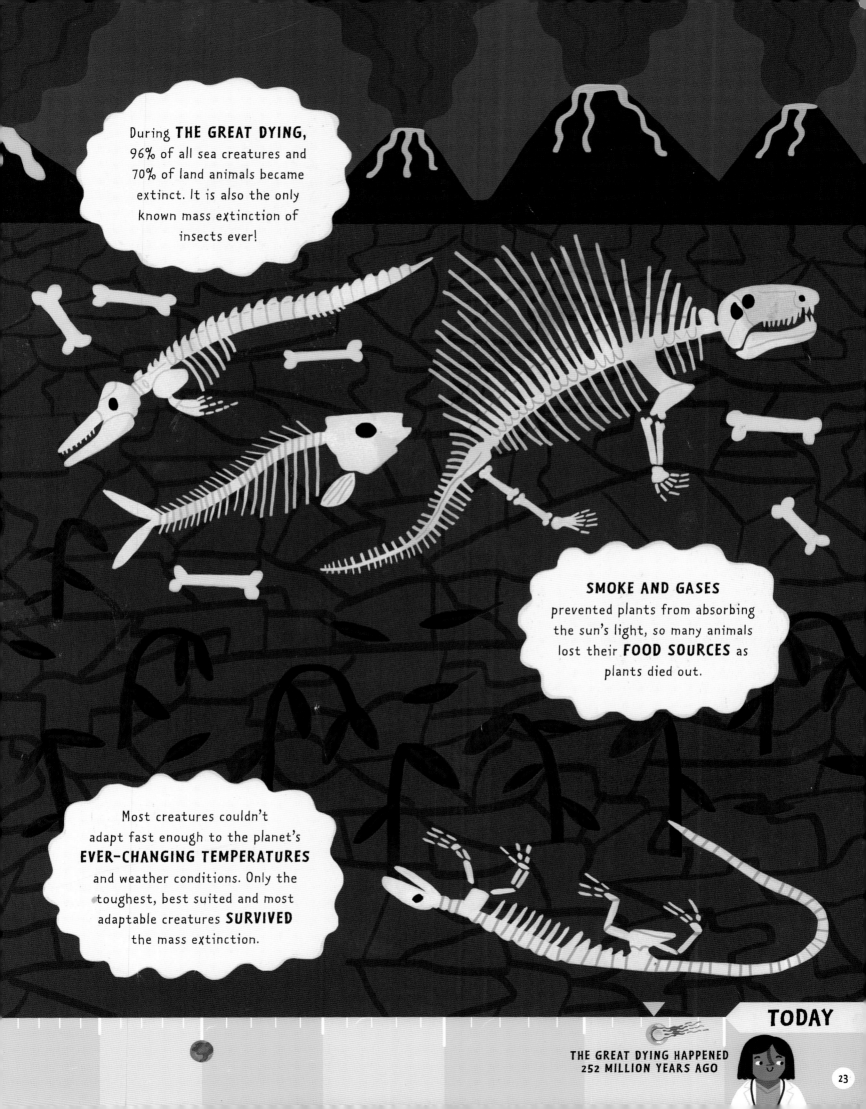

During **THE GREAT DYING**, 96% of all sea creatures and 70% of land animals became extinct. It is also the only known mass extinction of insects ever!

SMOKE AND GASES prevented plants from absorbing the sun's light, so many animals lost their **FOOD SOURCES** as plants died out.

Most creatures couldn't adapt fast enough to the planet's **EVER-CHANGING TEMPERATURES** and weather conditions. Only the toughest, best suited and most adaptable creatures **SURVIVED** the mass extinction.

TODAY

THE GREAT DYING HAPPENED 252 MILLION YEARS AGO

THE GREAT AFTERMATH

For the next eight million years, Earth became almost entirely barren once again.

Life in the sea recovered a lot quicker, with many of its species surviving and repopulating. This is probably because living underwater helped to protect them from what was happening above the surface.

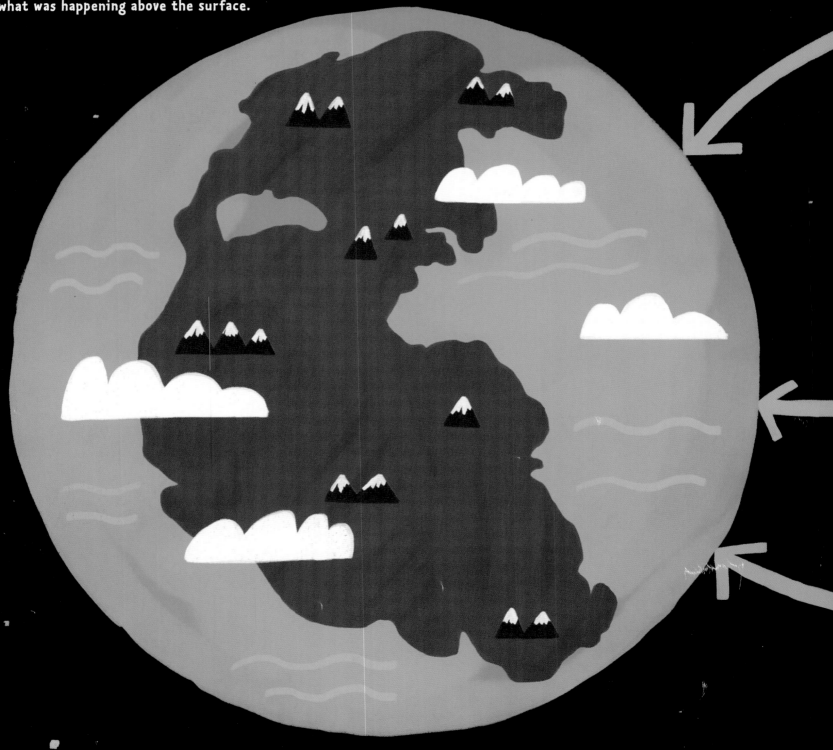

NATURAL DISASTERS

The climate remained unstable for a long time after the Great Dying and there may have been natural disasters and more mass extinctions in its aftermath. This all prevented life from recovering.

HOW TO SURVIVE

The smallest lifeforms had the best chance of survival, and during this time fungi, insects and mosses re-colonised the land and seas. Small creatures often reproduce quickly in very large numbers. They also need a lot less food to survive compared to bigger animals.

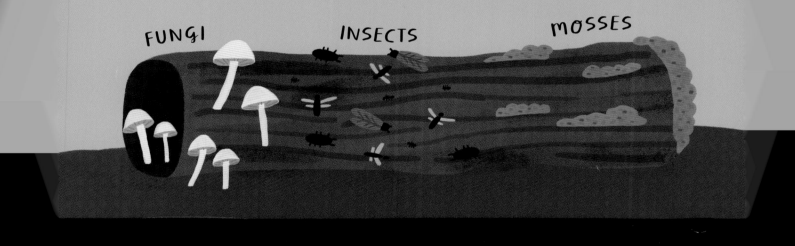

FUNGI   INSECTS   MOSSES

ADAPTABLE

The few species who survived this period were continually adapting to their new surroundings, and the devastating mass extinction ultimately led to a whole new collection of creatures evolving.

THE AGE OF DINOSAURS

The period after the Great Dying is called the Mesozoic Era or The Age of Dinosaurs! The first appearance of dinosaurs (which means 'terrible lizard' in Greek) came about in the first part of the Mesozoic Era – the Triassic period. But before the dinosaurs were the archosaurs.

MESOZOIC ERA

TRIASSIC PERIOD	JURASSIC PERIOD	CRETACEOUS PERIOD

252 million years ago   201 million years ago   145 million years ago   66 million years ago

ARCHOSAURS

The direct ancestors of dinosaurs were reptiles called archosaurs. These were the group of diapsids that survived the Great Dying and continued to evolve.

Archosaurs were so suited to Earth's conditions that they pretty much ruled the world at the start of the Triassic period – archosaur means 'ruling lizard'. Some examples of archosaurs are the short Proterosuchus and the nimble Euparkeria.

> I may be short but I rule the land!

PROTEROSUCHUS

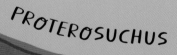

The **PROTEROSUCHUS** was an archosaur who looked a lot like a primitive crocodile. It walked on four stubby, sprawling legs.

TIMELINE

EUPARKERIA

EUPARKERIA

From these archosaurs evolved reptiles like the cat-sized **EUPARKERIA**. It walked on all fours but could stand up on its strong back legs if it needed to.

TRIASSIC PERIOD

The Triassic period lasted from 252 to 201 million years ago. A lot of changes happened during this time, including the evolution of dinosaurs and mammals.

The first dinosaurs, like the **EORAPTOR** and **NYASASAURUS**, appeared in the early to mid Triassic period.

PLEUROMEIA

EORAPTOR

NYASASAURUS

Some Triassic plants lived in moist ground near coasts or rivers. **PLEUROMEIA** was a small tree-like plant that had grassy leaves sprouting out from a single trunk. The drier parts of the world were more suited to conifers, ginkgoes and ferns.

TIMELINE

PTEROSAURS

Not all reptiles walked or swam – some could fly! Pterosaurs were flying reptiles that evolved in the Triassic and flew over dinosaurs for the whole Mesozoic Era. One type of pterosaur was EUDIMORPHODON. At about 70 cm in length, it had a long, bony tail, skin-covered wings and lots of sharp, small teeth!

EUDIMORPHODON

It was during the Triassic period that the first mammals began to evolve. The **MEGAZOSTRODON** was an early mammal that had lots of different sized teeth and was probably covered in fur for warmth.

MEGAZOSTRODON

PLACERIAS

Early dinosaurs shared the planet with large synpasids – the ancestors of mammals – like the **PLACERIAS**. It looked like a cross between a hog, a cow and a turtle. It was a large herbivore with a beak and pointed tusks that it used to dig for edible roots.

TODAY

THE TRIASSIC PERIOD LASTED FROM 252–201 MILLION YEARS AGO

DINOSAUR GROWTH

As dinsoaurs roamed Earth, they adapted and evolved to become bigger . . . and bigger . . . **and bigger!**

EORAPTOR

Middle Triassic period:
around 1 metre long

HERRERASAURUS

Late Triassic period:
3-6 metres long

DESMATOSUCHUS

Late Triassic period:
3-5 metres long

Late Triassic period:
4-6 metres long

POSTOSUCHUS

PLATEOSAURUS

Late Triassic period:
7-10 metres long

JURASSIC PERIOD

The Jurassic period lasted from around 201 to 145 million years ago. Many new and spectacular species of dinosaurs began to flourish during this time – this was when dinosaurs truly ruled the Earth.

GONDWANA

LAURASIA

THE END OF PANGAEA

During the Jurassic period, Pangaea started to break apart into two separate land masses: **LAURASIA** in the north and **GONDWANA** in the south. The Atlantic Ocean began to take form, and ocean winds brought rain to the desert areas. The temperature on Earth became milder than before, and life began to thrive in once barren areas.

SAUROPODS

The Jurassic period saw the appearance of giant plant-eating sauropods like the Brachiosaurus, Seismosaurus and Diplodocus. Sauropod means 'lizard foot' in Greek. Sauropods had very long necks, long tails, small heads and four thick, pillar-like legs.

Some sauropods, like **DIPLODOCUS**, probably swallowed small stones to help break down tough plant fibres in their stomach.

BRACHIOSAURUS ate leaves from the tops of trees. Its long neck may have developed so they could feed where other herbivores could not reach.

BRACHIOSAURUS

DIPLODOCUS

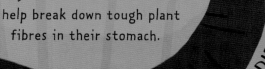

OTHER PLANT-EATERS

Another herbivore, the **STEGOSAURUS**, had armour for protection. It had two rows of backplates that ended in two pairs of spikes on the end of its tail. Although this looked very intimidating, stegosaurus was very slow moving and not too smart. In fact, for its body size, it had one of the smallest brains of all the dinosaurs!

STEGOSAURUS

Who are you calling stupid?

DRYOSAURUS

SCUTTELOSAURUS

Along with the larger herbivorous dinosaurs, there were tons of other small plant-eating dinosaurs running around. The **DRYOSAURUS** with its parrot-like beak and the **SCUTTELLOSAURUS** with its spike-covered body both lived during the Jurassic period.

ALLOSAURUS

DILOPHOSAURUS

DILOPHOSAURUS was a big two-legged hunter with a bony crest on its skull, which was used either to impress a mate or to cool itself down.

MEAT-EATERS

Large meat-eating predators such as **ALLOSAURUS** and **DILOPHOSAURUS** also emerged at this time. Allosaurus used its sharp sense of smell to find prey and pounce on them! They had three clawed fingers which were perfect for grasping.

TODAY

THE JURASSIC PERIOD LASTED FROM 201 TO 145 MILLION YEARS AGO

33

CRETACEOUS PERIOD

The Cretaceous period began 145 million years ago. The continents started to move into the positions and shapes that we recognise today. Some parts of the Earth flooded, making shallow seas that flowed over land. The first flowering plants began to grow. On each continent, dinosaurs developed in very different ways...

HADROSAURS had a crest on their heads, like **PARASAUROLOPHUS** or **CORYTHOSAURUS**. They were herbivores and grazed on leaves, ferns and bark in large herds, a lot like cows.

PARASAUROLOPHUS

CORYTHOSAURUS

PROTOCERATOPS

CERATOPSIANS were the 'horned face' dinosaurs, and these included **PROTOCERATOPS** and the famous **TRICERATOPS**. These herbivores had parrot-like beaks and were built a lot like rhinos.

TRICERATOPS

GASTONIA

EDMONTONIA

ANKYLOSAURS were the armoured tanks of the dinosaur world. Some had spines on their bodies like **EDMONTONIA**, some had spiky tails like **GASTONIA** and some had bony clubs at the end of their tails like **ANKYLOSAURUS**!

ANKYLOSAURUS

TIMELINE

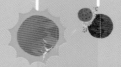

The mighty **TYRANNOSAURUS REX** is one of the most well-known carnivorous dinosaurs. It was over 12 metres long and four metres tall!

TYRANNOSAURUS REX

Its strong jaws and razor-sharp teeth (each as long as a human hand) meant that it could kill and eat anything it wanted, placing it very firmly at the top of the food chain. It had short arms to grab at prey, and long thin legs to help it sprint.

VELOCIRAPTOR

DROMAEOSAURIDS were bird-like dinosaurs that were probably covered with feathers for warmth. These carnivorous dinosaurs had sharp claws for attacking prey. They include **DEINONYCHUS**, which by dinosaur standards had a large brain, and **VELOCIRAPTOR**, an aggressive and fast predator that was the size of a large turkey.

DEINONYCHUS

ARGENTINOSAURUS

The biggest dinosaur of them all was a sauropod called **ARGENTINOSAURUS**. Like the other sauropods that went before it, Argentinosaurus had a long neck and long tail, small head, and four thick, pillar-like legs. It is thought to have been 30 metres long and weighed 100 tons – that's about ten T-rexes!

TODAY

THE CRETACEOUS PERIOD LASTED FROM 145–66 MILLION YEARS AGO

DINOSAUR DIETS AND ANATOMY

Dinosaur diets can tell us lots about how different species of dinosaur adapted to suit their environment. Dinosaurs that ate the meat of other species are called carnivores, and those that survived solely on vegetation are called herbivores. Omnivores ate a mixture of meat and plants.

Is it lunchtime yet?

HIPS

There are two types of hip bones in the dinosaur kingdom: bird hips and lizard hips.

LIZARD HIPS

BIRD HIPS

Most meat-eating dinosaurs, as well as the large sauropods, were lizard-hipped. Lizard hips may have helped carnivores to run fast and hunt down prey.

The plant-eaters were mainly bird-hipped. These hips slanted in a certain way that may have helped to make room for the large intestines necessary for digesting plants.

CLAWS

Meat-eating dinosaurs had sharp, hooked claws used for attacking and eating their prey. They are called therapods, which means 'beast-footed'.

Plant-eaters had blunt claws or hooves to protect their feet as they trudged great distances to find their favourite leafy meal.

There are many different tooth types in the dinosaur world, each made for unique tasks. Most carnivores had teeth designed for slicing through flesh or crunching bones.

Herbivores had flatter teeth designed for grinding through leaves and mashing vegetation into a pulp.

STOMACH AND INTESTINES

Meat-eaters' digestive juices dissolved meat and even bones in their stomachs.

Plant-eaters had much longer intestines for digesting enormous amounts of plants.

EGGS

As a general rule, eggs laid by meat-eating dinosaurs were usually much longer than they were wide, like a rugby ball.

Eggs laid by plant-eaters tended to be more spherical, like a football.

DINOSAUR FAMILY TREE

Just like you and I can trace our ancestors by drawing a family tree, dinosaurs can be linked together to show how different species are related to each other. Each type of dinosaur is called a species, and one or more closely related species make up a genus. A species, together with all of its descendants, forms a group called a clade.

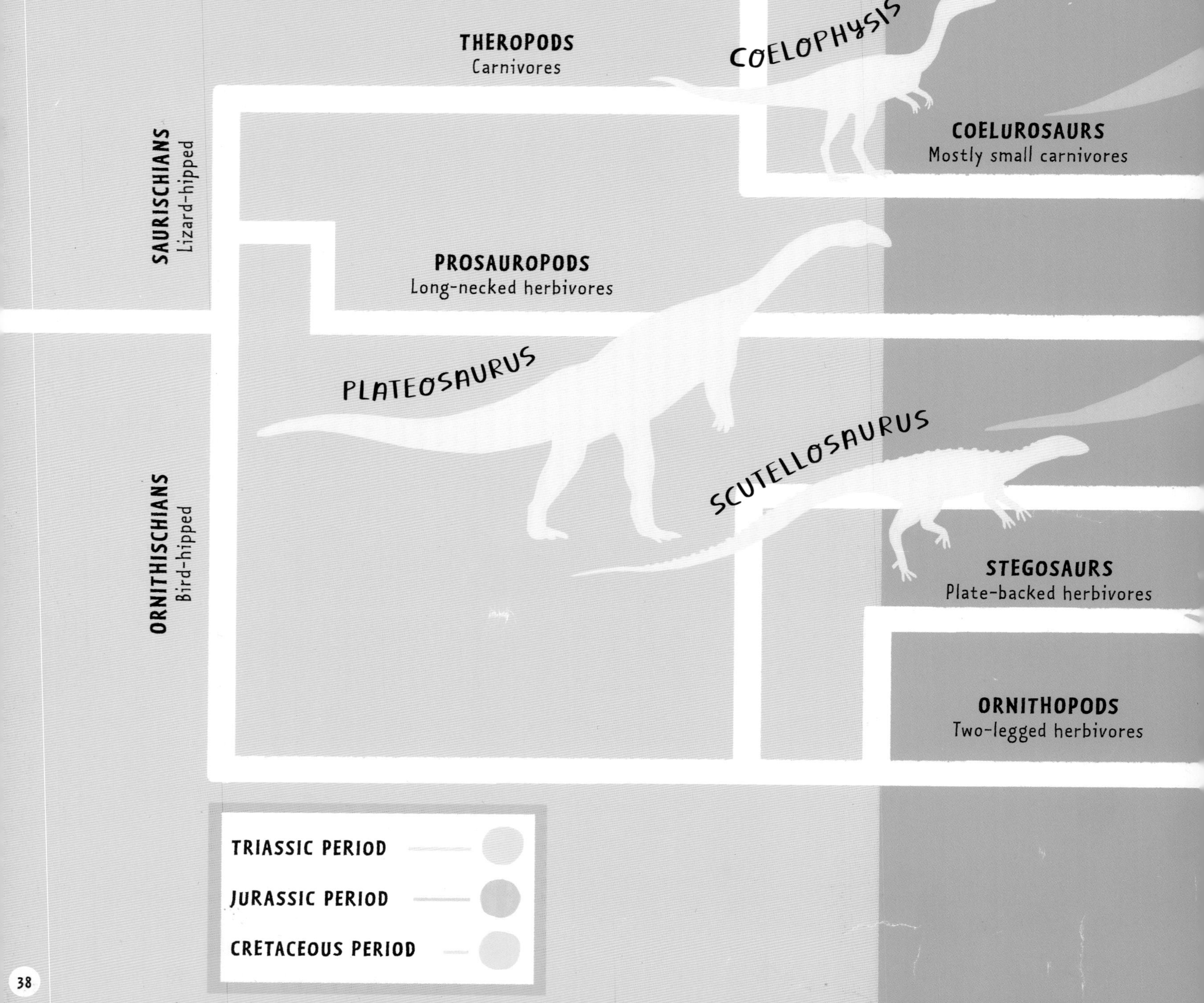

CARNOSAURS
Mostly large carnivores

THEROPODS
Carnivores

COELOPHYSIS

COELUROSAURS
Mostly small carnivores

SAURISCHIANS
Lizard-hipped

PROSAUROPODS
Long-necked herbivores

PLATEOSAURUS

SCUTELLOSAURUS

ORNITHISCHIANS
Bird-hipped

STEGOSAURS
Plate-backed herbivores

ORNITHOPODS
Two-legged herbivores

TRIASSIC PERIOD ⚫

JURASSIC PERIOD ⚫

CRETACEOUS PERIOD ⚫

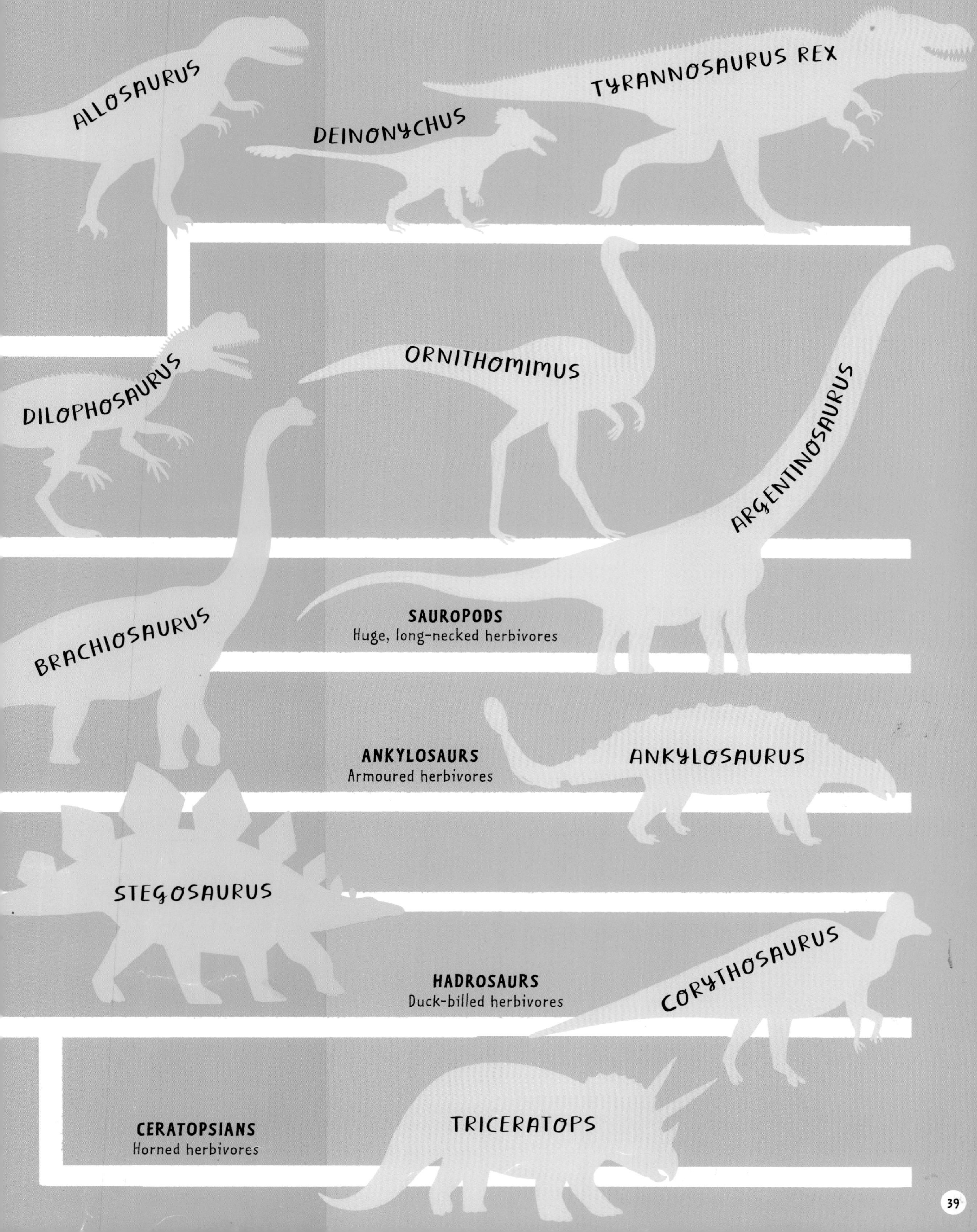

ALLOSAURUS

DEINONYCHUS

TYRANNOSAURUS REX

DILOPHOSAURUS

ORNITHOMIMUS

ARGENTINOSAURUS

BRACHIOSAURUS

SAUROPODS
Huge, long-necked herbivores

ANKYLOSAURS
Armoured herbivores

ANKYLOSAURUS

STEGOSAURUS

HADROSAURS
Duck-billed herbivores

CORYTHOSAURUS

CERATOPSIANS
Horned herbivores

TRICERATOPS

MAMMALS

Small, furry mammals first appeared in the Triassic period and continued to develop during the Jurassic and Cretaceous periods. They existed alongside dinosaurs for millions of years.

I'm an example of a modern mammal.

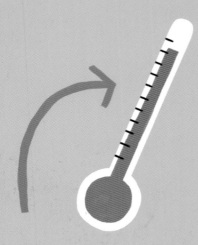

Mammals are warm-blooded animals. They keep their bodies warm whether it is cold outside or not, unlike cold-blooded creatures who need the sun to heat themselves.

Mammals live in lots of different habitats, such as oceans, underground, tree tops and deserts. They can be carnivores, omnivores or herbivores.

Mammals are vertebrates that feed their young on their milk. Most mammals have fur or hair and give birth to live babies, as opposed to laying eggs and waiting for them to hatch.

The very early mammals appeared around 220 million years ago and were tiny! The Triassic **EOZOSTRODON**, the Jurassic **JURAMAIA** and the Cretaceous **ALPHADON** all resembled rodents, with long thin tails and sharp claws for burrowing. They probably were nocturnal, feasting on insects and dinosaur eggs in the dark to avoid being caught by dinosaurs!

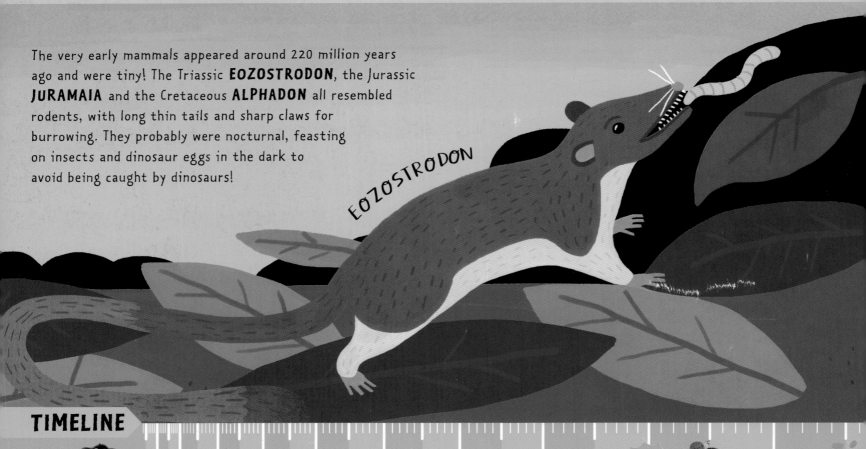

EOZOSTRODON

TIMELINE

ALPHADON was a type of mammal called a MARSUPIAL, which carry their young in a pouch like a kangaroo!

ALPHADON

Hello!

JURAMAIA

Another mammal from the Cretaceous period was the STEROPODON. It was a lot like a platypus. It was a very unusual mammal because it laid eggs instead of giving birth to live young.

STEROPODON

TODAY

THE FIRST MAMMALS APPEARED 220 MILLION YEARS AGO

BIRDS

The earliest known birds first appeared in the Jurassic period around 150 million years ago. Surprisingly, birds did not evolve from pterosaurs, the flying lizards who filled the skies from the late Triassic to the end of the Cretaceous period. They evolved from theropods – the two-legged, tree-climbing, feathered dinosaurs! These agile predators developed wings over millions of years – first to help them chase and leap after their prey and, ultimately, to fly.

QUETZALCOATLUS

QUETZALCOATLUS, a pterodactyl, was one of the largest flying animals of all time, with a wingspan of eleven metres! It had a long sharp beak, four legs and a huge flap of skin that stretched over its front legs and acted as wings for flying.

BIRD EVOLUTION

AURORNIS XUI was a small feathered dinosaur that lived 160 million years ago. It looked like a ground bird, but with a long tail, clawed hands and toothed jaws. Although some scientists believe it is the earliest known bird, most agree that it is one of the dinosaurs that birds evolved from.

AURORNIS XUI

Feathers don't just look pretty, they contain oils to protect birds from getting wet and insulate them from cold weather.

THE FIRST BIRD

ARCHAEOPTERYX lived around 150 million years ago and had the toothed head, long tail, and clawed hands of a dinosaur. It was covered in feathers and was about the size of a pigeon. Its name means 'first wing', and it is thought to be the oldest known bird.

ARCHAEOPTERYX

TODAY

BIRDS FIRST EVOLVED 150 MILLION YEARS AGO

MASS EXTINCTION

Earth had changed so much from the Big Bang up to this point. Over millions of years, it became home to an amazing array of mammals, birds, dinosaurs, plants and fish. But, terrible mass extinction hit Earth again, around 66 million years ago, when an enormous rock came hurtling through space and crashed into the sea near the Yucatan Peninsula in modern-day Mexico.

The deadly asteroid was at least ten kilometres wide, which is bigger than 100 football pitches end to end! It exploded when it hit Earth, creating a huge cloud of dust and toxic fumes that spread across the world.

TIMELINE

This poisonous cloud suffocated animals and blocked the sun's light and warmth from plants. When the vegetation perished, herbivores starved to death and this meant that carnivores had nothing to eat either, just like what happened in the Great Dying, 186 million years before.

The mighty dinosaurs were completely wiped out in the mass extinction. Fossils show us that Triceratops and T-Rex were two of the last surviving dinosaurs.

TODAY

ASTEROID CAUSES MASS EXTINCTION 66 MILLION YEARS AGO

DARKNESS

Earth sat in complete darkness for almost two whole years and half of all living species died.

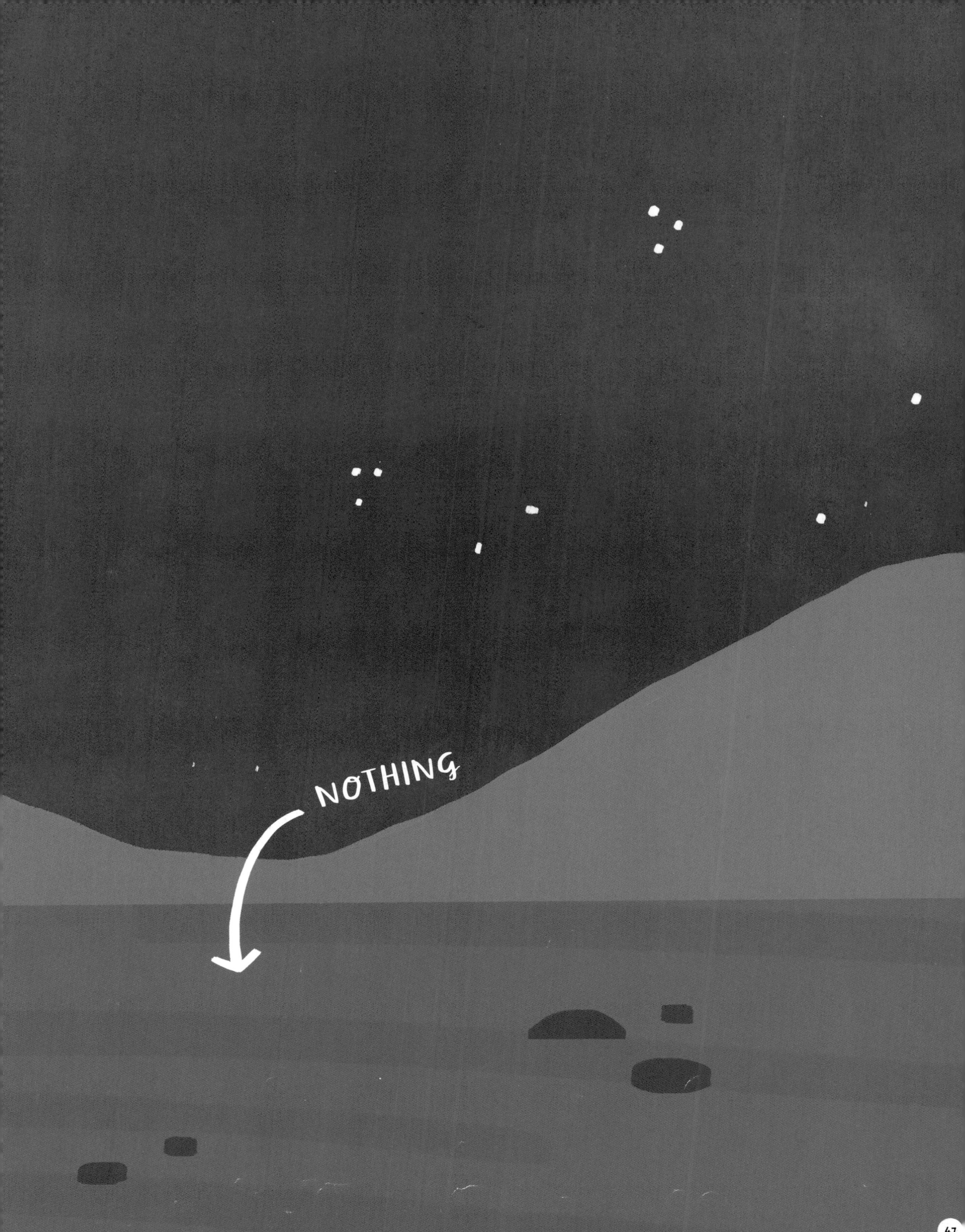
NOTHING

WHO SURVIVED?

Not all animals suffered the same fate as the now-extinct dinosaurs. Animals that ate a varied diet of roots, seeds and insects, as well as decaying plants and other animals, had a better chance of survival and adapted to these new conditions.

I'm a survivor!

CROCODILES AND ALLIGATORS

CRABS

TURTLES

BIRDS

LIZARDS

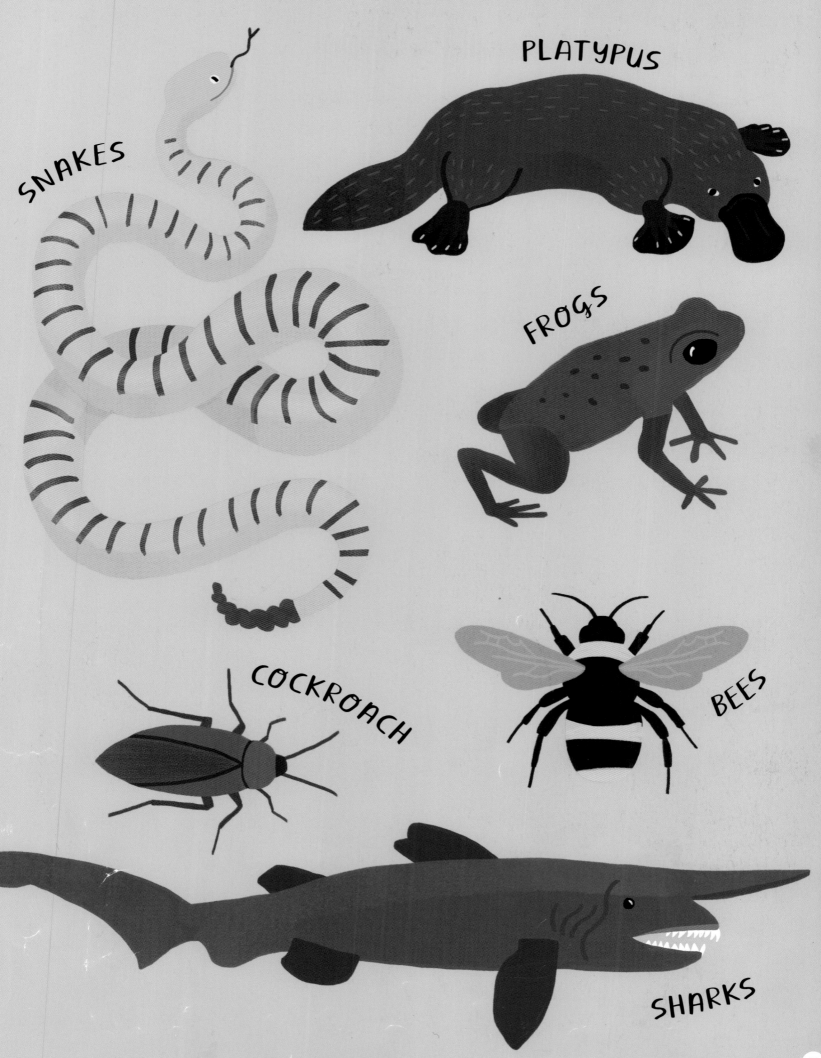

SNAKES

PLATYPUS

FROGS

COCKROACH

BEES

SHARKS

THE AGE OF MAMMALS

When the dust settled and the atmosphere cleared, the Cenozoic Era, or 'The Age of Mammals', began, which is the same geological era we are in today. The surviving mammals on Earth evolved even further, becoming more and more diverse. Today, there are three main groups of mammals and many subgroups, including carnivora, ungulates, cetacea, rodentia, chiroptera and primates.

MIACID

I eat meat but I also like berries and nuts!

CARNIVORA

CARNIVORA originally developed to hunt and eat meat, like **MIACIDS** which lived from 62 million years ago. Although most are mainly carnivorous, some have evolved into omnivores and some, such as pandas, are entirely herbivorous. Cats, dogs, seals and bears are all members of this group.

RODENTS

PHOBEROMYS PATTERSONI

RODENTS account for around 40% of all mammal species! They have large incisors which they use for gnawing. Mice, rats, beavers and squirrels are all rodents. **PHOBEROMYS PATTERSONI** was a rodent that lived in South America nine million years ago. At over 1.5 metres tall, it resembled a *very* large capybara!

TIMELINE

UNGULATES are hoofed mammals. There are odd-toed ungulates, like horses and rhinos, and even-toed ungulates, like deer, giraffes and hippos. **HYRACOTHERIUM**, which looked like a dog-sized horse, was an early odd-toed ungulate that lived 55 million years ago. **ENTELODONTS** were early even-toed ungulates that lived 37 million years ago and looked like tall, bulky hogs, hence their nickname 'terminator pigs'.

ENTELODONT

UNGULATES

HYRACOTHERIUM

CETACEA evolved from the even-toed ungulates. These are sea-dwelling mammals like whales and dolphins. **AMBULOCETUS** was an ancestor to whales, although it may not look much like one! These 'walking whales' were about the size of a sea lion and had long jaws like a crocodile. They lived near Pakistan around 46 million years ago.

AMBULOCETUS

CETACEA

CHIROPTERA

PALAEOCHIROPTERYX

Bats might look a bit like rodents, but they belong to their own group called **CHIROPTERA**. They are the only mammals capable of flying. **PALAEOCHIROPTERYX** is an extinct bat that lived in Germany 48 million years ago. Well-preserved fossils of these bats show us that they had reddish-brown fur and short, broad wings.

TODAY

THE AGE OF MAMMALS BEGINS 66 MILLION YEARS AGO

PRIMATES

Primates first appeared on Earth around 65 to 55 million years ago. Unlike a lot of other mammals, they have large brains compared to their body size. They have forward-facing eyes to help them judge distances well. Many primates have opposable thumbs too. This means their thumb moves in the opposite direction to their fingers, allowing their hand to grip. There are a number of groups of primates including lemurs, bushbabies, monkeys, apes and humans.

Lemurs and bushbabies are primates with small brains, wet noses and special teeth used for grooming their fur!

ARCHAEOINDRIS

MOUSE LEMUR

LEMURS live exclusively on the African island of Madagascar. They are a diverse bunch ranging from the tiny mouse lemur to the famous ring-tailed lemur. **ARCHAEOINDRIS** is an extinct giant lemur the size of a male gorilla!

BUSHBABY

RING-TAILED LEMUR

BUSHBABIES are small, nocturnal primates, found in Africa. They have huge eyes for seeing at night and bat-like ears for tracking insects in the dark. The earliest primates would have been more like bushbabies than monkeys.

TIMELINE

BABOON

Tarsiers, apes and monkeys have large brains and dry noses.

TARSIER

The oldest **TARSIER** fossils are 45 million years old and show they've changed very little since that time! Small with huge eyes — each eyeball is as large as their brain — they hunt by leaping at prey from a perch. They are the only entirely carnivorous primate, feasting on insects and sometimes lizards, birds or snakes.

CAPUCHIN MONKEY

MANDRILL

SPIDER MONKEY

MONKEYS have a tail and live in trees. They use their nimble hands for tasks like peeling fruit. Monkeys that live in Africa and Asia, like baboons or mandrills, are called Old World monkeys and those in Central and South America, like capuchin or squirrel monkeys, are called New World monkeys.

TODAY

PRIMATES FIRST APPEARED 65-55 MILLION YEARS AGO

APES

Apes are another group of animals that belong to the primate family. They first appeared on Earth 20 million years ago, and are divided into the 'Great Apes' and the 'Lesser Apes'.

GREAT APES

The GREAT APES include chimpanzees, bonobos, gorillas, orangutans and humans. They are all tall and tailless, and mostly omnivorous. Great apes can use their nimble hands to gather things, feed and even use tools. They build nests on the ground or in treetops. Many reuse old nests but some, such as gorillas, make a new nest every night for that fresh feeling!

CHIMPANZEE

CHIMPANZEES are the primate most similar to humans, sharing 99% of human DNA. This makes chimps more similar to humans than mice are to rats! Just like humans, chimps use many different facial expressions to show each other how they're feeling.

PLAYFUL

SCARED

EXCITED

WHAT IS DNA?
DNA is the molecule that contains an organism's genetic code, which is the basic instructions for how a living thing develops and lives. It is short for deoxyribonucleic acid.

TIMELINE

GORILLAS are the largest of all the great apes. They might look scary, but typically they are gentle and shy, spending most of their time on the ground eating leaves and berries. They walk on all fours with their knuckles on the ground.

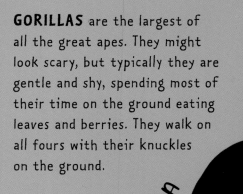

GORILLA

ORANGUTAN

ORANGUTANS live in rainforests in Southeast Asia. They are the world's biggest tree-dwellers and can quickly move around the forest canopy using their strong hands and feet.

I like to be hugged

BONOBO

BONOBOS are about the same size as chimpanzees but have a smaller head and longer arms. They have a black face with pink lips, wide nostrils, and long hair on their heads that forms a parting! They like to touch, hug and groom each other to make friends.

GIBBON

LESSER APES

Lesser Apes, also simply known as Gibbons, are much smaller than great apes and they spend almost all their time in trees. They don't build nests; instead, they sleep sitting upright on branches! Gibbons have long arms and use their hands like hooks to move from branch to branch, sometimes up to 35 miles per hour! They are known for singing loud songs in the early morning and late afternoon to keep others out of their territory.

TODAY

APES FIRST APPEARED 20 MILLION YEARS AGO

HUMAN EVOLUTION

Scientists have discovered fossils of ancient apes that show us how humans evolved from these primates over millions of years. Oreopithecus was a human-like ape that lived around 8 million years ago. We can see how, over time, the species that followed evolved to more closely resemble humans.

Look! I'm walking on two legs!

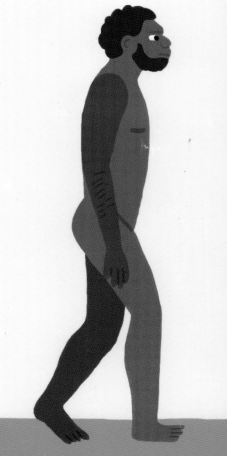

OREOPITHECUS
9 to 7 million years ago

AUSTRALOPITHECUS AFARENSIS
3.9 to 2.9 million years ago

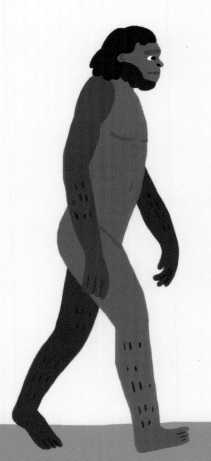

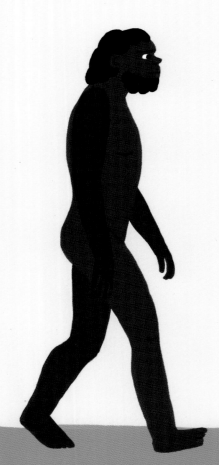

HOMO ERECTUS
1.8 to 0.2 million years ago

SOLO MAN
subspecies of Homo Erectus
0.5 million years ago

HOMO HEIDELBERGENSIS
0.5 to 0.2 million years ago

PARANTHROPUS

2.6 to 1.1 million years ago

AUSTRALOPITHECUS
SEDIBA

2 to 1.5 million years ago

HOMO NEANDERTHALENSIS

0.4 to 0.04 million years ago

MODERN HOMO
SAPIENS

EARLY HUMANS

Hominins are the group of primates that include modern and extinct humans and their immediate ancestors.

AUSTRALOPITHECUS AFARENSIS, which means 'southern ape', was an early hominin that lived in African grasslands alongside elephants, rhinos and giraffes 3.9 to 2.9 million years ago. They looked similar to apes, with a flat nose, a brain much smaller than modern humans, and long, strong arms with curved fingers for climbing trees. They also had black fur that covered their heads and bodies. But they had some similarities to modern humans too. They walked upright on two feet, keeping their arms free for other tasks like carrying and throwing things. Standing upright also had other benefits, like running fast over long distances and seeing above tall grasses to spot danger.

The most famous Australopithecus afarensis is a fossilised skeleton called Lucy, who got her name from The Beatles' song 'Lucy in the Sky with Diamonds'. She was 110 centimetres tall, weighed 29 kilograms and looked a bit like a chimpanzee.

TIMELINE

NEANDERTHALS were hominins that looked very similar to modern humans but were shorter and much stronger. They had a strong, ridged brow and a large nose. They lived in caves in Europe and Asia during the Ice Ages, about 300,000 years ago, and wore simple clothes made from animal fur to protect them from the cold.

TODAY

EARLY HOMININS APPEARED 3.9 MILLION YEARS AGO

MODERN HUMANS

You, me and every person you'll ever meet belongs to one group of primates – Homo sapiens, which means 'wise man'. Modern humans that looked like us appeared on Earth about 200,000 years ago.

By about 28,000 years ago, Neanderthals had died out and Homo sapiens were the only humans left on the planet. They began to occupy every continent on Earth! Over this time, humans developed different cultures, languages, rituals and ways of life. Millions of years of evolution, extinctions and survival led to this very moment — you, a primate of the Chordate phylum, reading about how you came to be. And it all started with a ball of energy smaller than this full stop.

BLOOMSBURY CHILDREN'S BOOKS
Bloomsbury Publishing Plc
50 Bedford Square, London, WC1B 3DP, UK

BLOOMSBURY, BLOOMSBURY CHILDREN'S BOOKS and the Diana logo are trademarks of Bloomsbury Publishing Plc

First published in Great Britain 2020 by Bloomsbury Publishing Plc
Text and illustrations copyright © Kathi Burke, 2020

A catalogue record for this book is available from the British Library

ISBN: 978-1-4088-9861-1

2 4 6 8 10 9 7 5 3 1

Printed and bound in India by Replika Press Pvt. Ltd

All papers used by Bloomsbury Publishing Plc are natural, recyclable products from wood
grown in well managed forests. The manufacturing processes conform to the
environmental regulations of the country of origin

To find out more about our authors and books visit www.bloomsbury.com
and sign up for our newsletters

'THE AGE OF DINOSAURS' BEGINS
252 MILLION YEARS AGO

THE FIRST BIRDS
EVOLVE 150 MILLION
YEARS AGO

THE FIRST MAMMALS
EVOLVE 220 MILLION
YEARS AGO

'THE GREAT DYING' MASS
EXTINCTION HAPPENS 252
MILLION YEARS AGO